VOCAL/PIANO

ORIGINAL KEYS *for* **SINGERS**

LADIES of Christmas

ISBN 978-1-4584-0827-3

HAL•LEONARD®
CORPORATION

7777 W. BLUEMOUND RD. P.O. BOX 13819 MILWAUKEE, WI 53213

Visit Hal Leonard Online at
www.halleonard.com

CAROLING, CAROLING

Words by WIHLA HUTSON
Music by ALFRED BURT

Moderately slow, in 1

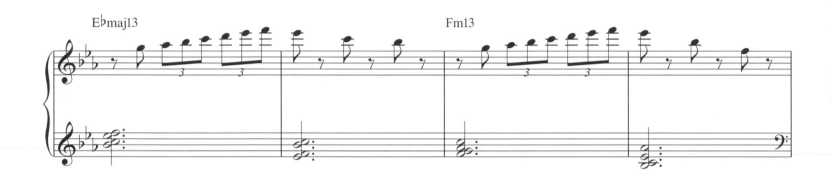

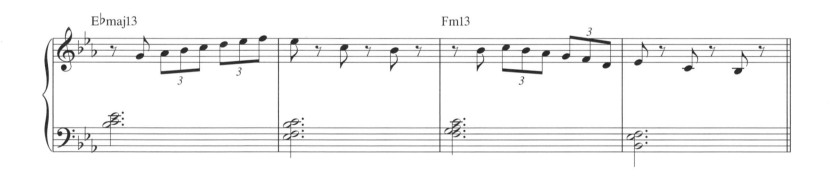

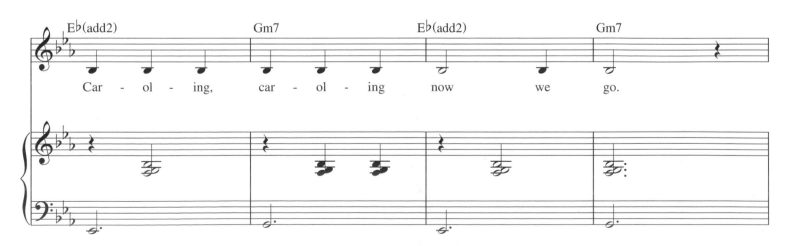

Car - ol - ing, car - ol - ing now we go.

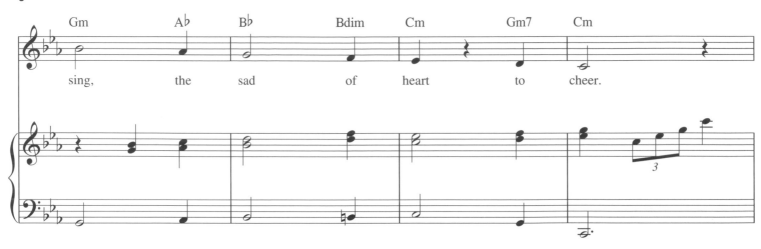

sing,   the   sad   of   heart   to   cheer.

Ding,   dong,   ding,   dong,

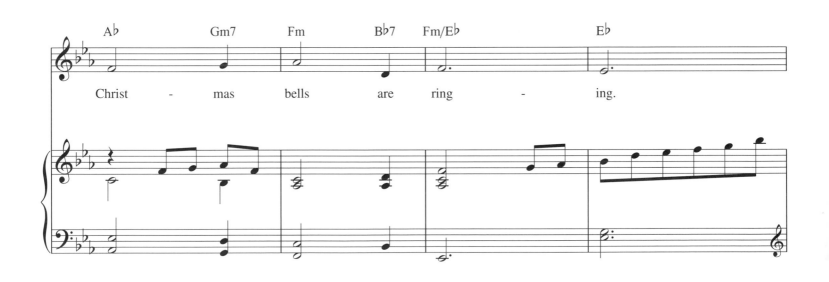

Christ - mas   bells   are   ring - ing.

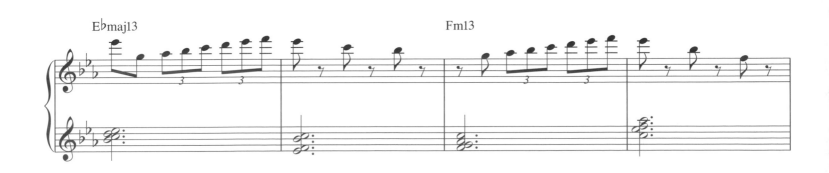

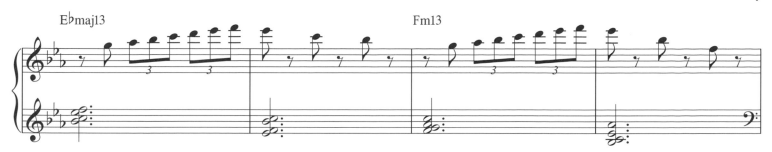

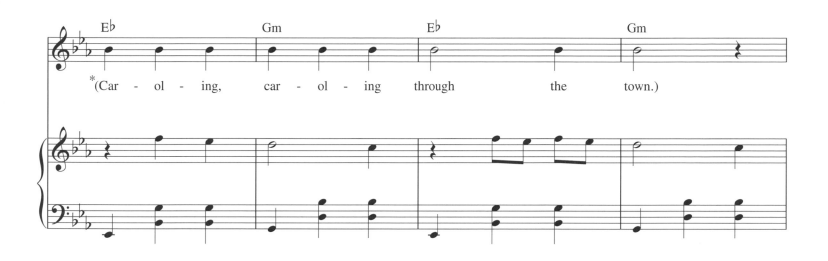

*(Car - ol - ing, car - ol - ing through the town.)

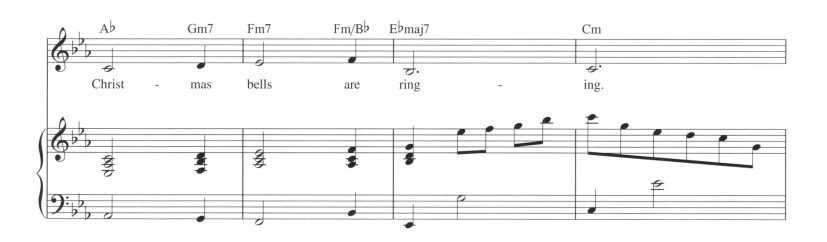

Christ - mas bells are ring - ing.

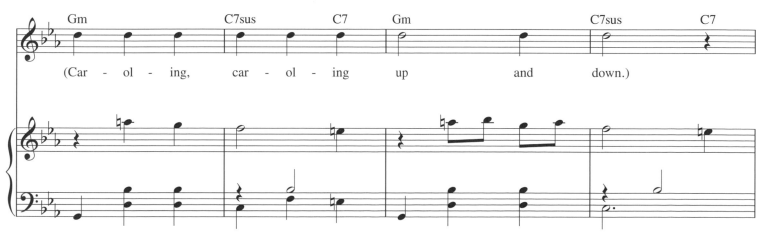

(Car - ol - ing, car - ol - ing up and down.)

*All background vocals sung by children's choir.

THE CHRISTMAS SONG
(Chestnuts Roasting On An Open Fire)

Music and Lyric by MEL TORME
and ROBERT WELLS

*Lead vocal written an octave higher than sung.

times, man - y ways, mer - ry Christ - mas, mer -

- ry Christ-mas, mer - ry Christ - mas to

you.

Spoken: Merry Christmas.

rit.

CHRISTMAS TIME IS HERE

from A CHARLIE BROWN CHRISTMAS

Words by Lee Mendelson
Music by VINCE GUARALDI

DO YOU HEAR WHAT I HEAR

Words and Music by NOEL REGNEY
and GLORIA SHAYNE

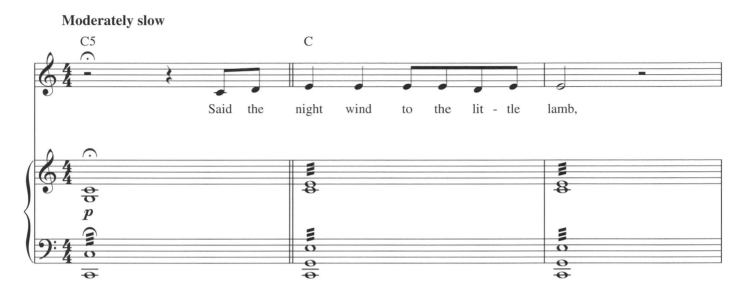

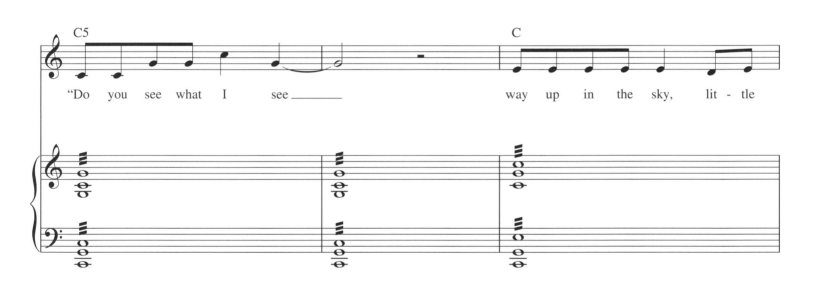

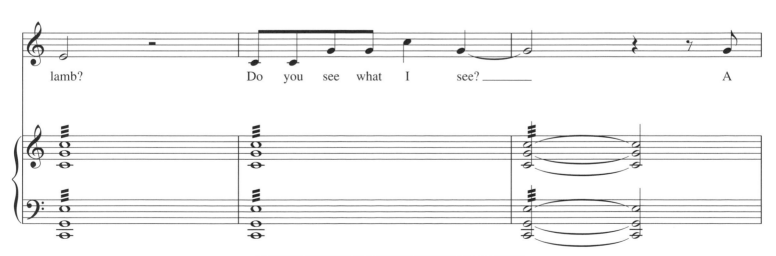

(Do you hear what I hear?) _____ Said the

shep-herd boy to the might-y king,

"Do you know what I know? _____ In your

pal - ace warm, _____ might - y king, _____ do you know what I know? _____ A child, a child _____ shiv - ers _____ in the cold. Let us bring Him sil - ver and gold. _____ Let us bring him sil - ver and

FELIZ NAVIDAD

Music and Lyrics by
JOSÉ FELICIANO

GROWN-UP CHRISTMAS LIST

Words and Music by DAVID FOSTER
and LINDA THOMPSON-JENNER

grown up _____ Christ-mas list, not for my-self,

but for a world in need: _____

Moderately, steadily

No more lives _____ torn a-part;

that wars _____ would nev-er start;

HALLELUJAH

Words and Music by
LEONARD COHEN

lu - jah.   Hal - le - lu - lu - jah.

1-3
- jah.
Well, your
Well,
Well, there

4
jah.

Well, may - be _____ there is a God a - bove, _____ but

Additional lyrics

There was a time when you let me know
What's really going on below,
But now you never show that to me, do you?
Well, I remember when I moved in you,
When the Holy Ghost was moving too,
And ev'ry breath we drew was "Hallelujah!"

HAPPY HOLIDAY

from the Motion Picture Irving Berlin's HOLIDAY INN

Words and Music by
IRVING BERLIN

HAPPY XMAS
(War Is Over)

Words and Music by JOHN LENNON
and YOKO ONO

Moderately slow, in 1

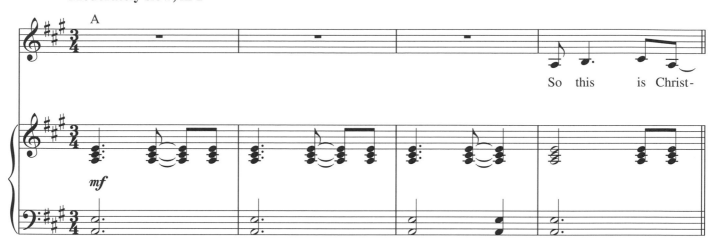

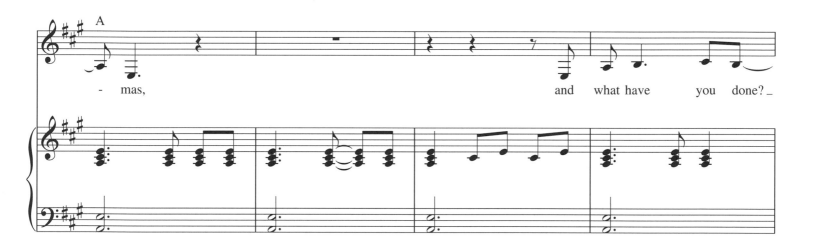

HARD CANDY CHRISTMAS

from THE BEST LITTLE WHOREHOUSE IN TEXAS

Words and Music by
CAROL HALL

HERE COMES SANTA CLAUS
(Right Down Santa Claus Lane)

Words and Music by GENE AUTRY
and OAKLEY HALDEMAN

Here comes San-ta Claus, here comes San-ta Claus

right down San-ta Claus Lane. Vix-en and Blit-zen and

all his rein-deer are pull-in' on the rein.

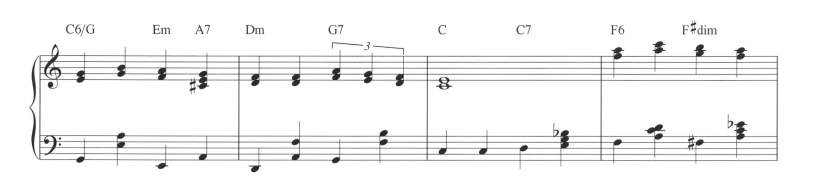

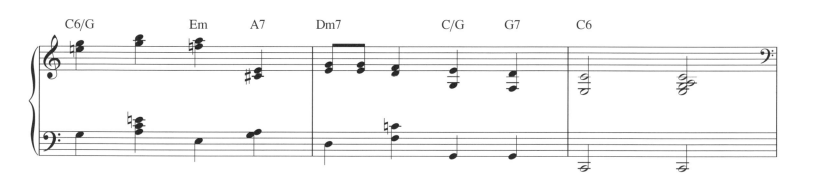

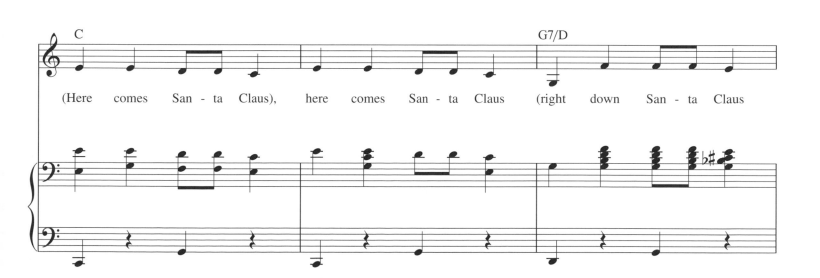

(Here comes San - ta Claus), here comes San - ta Claus (right down San - ta Claus

A HOLLY JOLLY CHRISTMAS

Music and Lyrics by
JOHNNY MARKS

Lyrics: Have a hol-ly, jol-ly Christ-mas. It's the best time of the year. ___

I HEARD THE BELLS ON CHRISTMAS DAY

Words by HENRY WADSWORTH LONGFELLOW
Adapted by JOHNNY MARKS
Music by JOHNNY MARKS

98

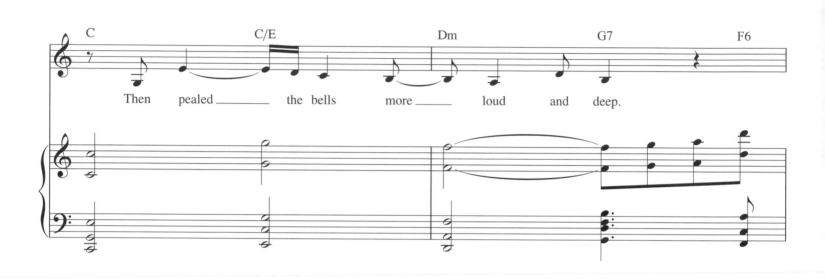

Then pealed _____ the bells more _____ loud and deep.

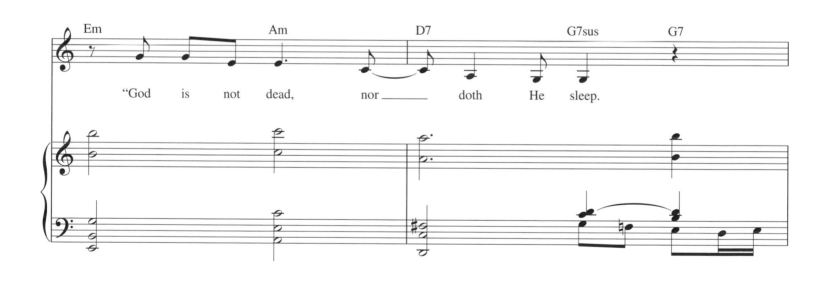

"God is not dead, nor _____ doth He sleep.

The wrong ___ shall ___ fail, The right _____ pre - vail, ___ With

I SAW MOMMY KISSING SANTA CLAUS

Words and Music by
TOMMIE CONNOR

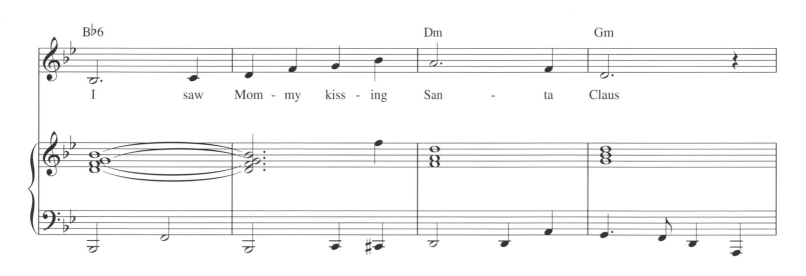

I saw Mom - my kiss - ing San - ta Claus

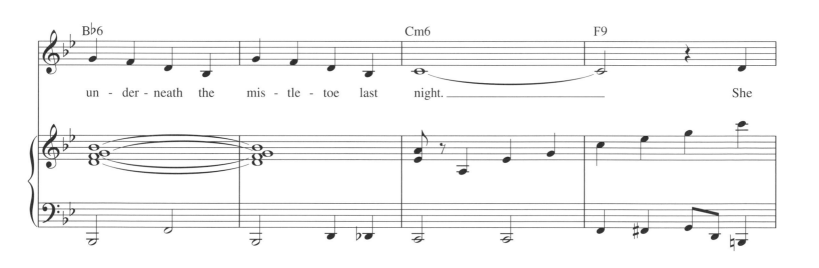

un - der - neath the mis - tle - toe last night. _____ She

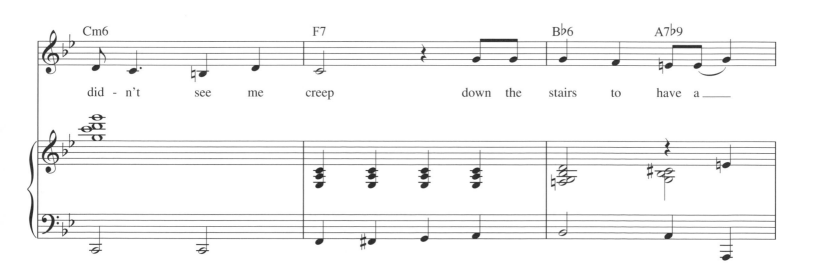

did - n't see me creep down the stairs to have a ____

I saw

I WONDER AS I WANDER

By JOHN JACOB NILES

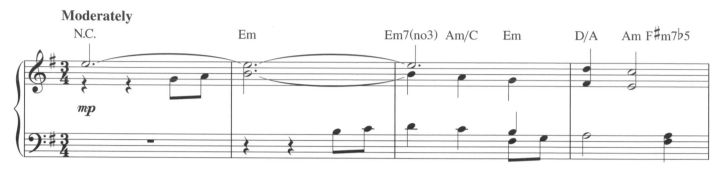

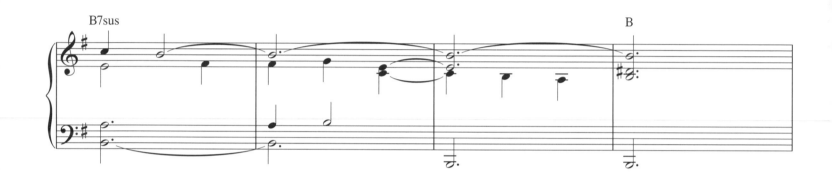

Pedal ad lib. throughout

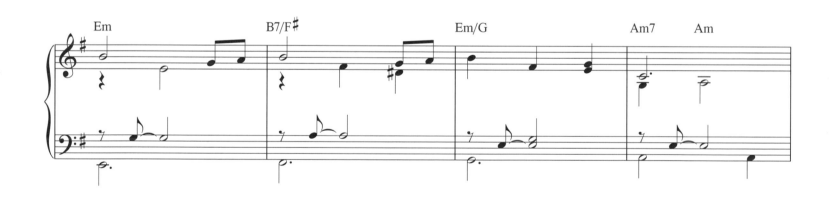

If

Je - sus had want - ed for an - y wee thing— a

star in the sky, or _____ a bird on _____ the wing or

all of God's an - gels in heav - en to sing— He

I'LL BE HOME FOR CHRISTMAS

Words and Music by KIM GANNON
and WALTER KENT

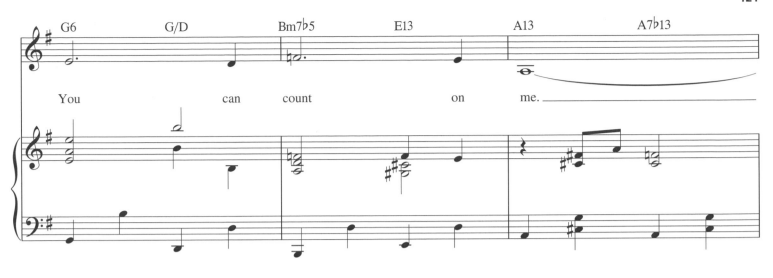

You can count on me. _____

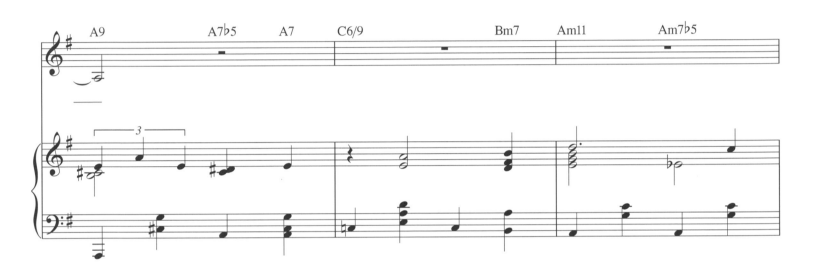

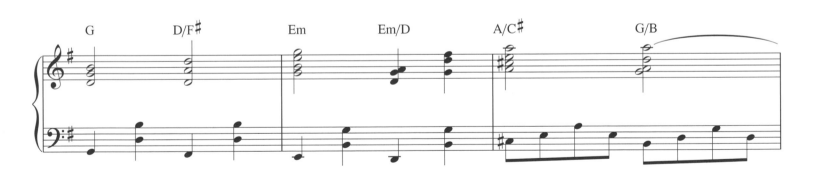

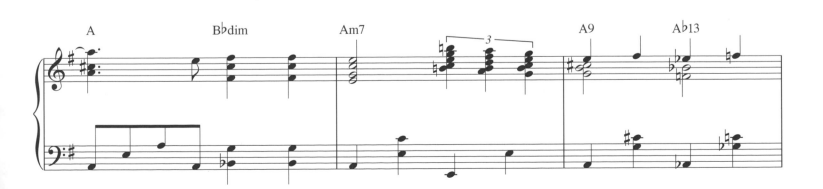

IT'S BEGINNING TO LOOK LIKE CHRISTMAS

By MEREDITH WILLSON

Sounding good, there.   Yeah,   y - yeah, __ yeah, ___

yeah _ ooh, __ ooh, __ ooh, ooh, oh, oh. _____   *(Lead vocal ad lib. to end)*

Repeat and Fade   **Optional Ending**

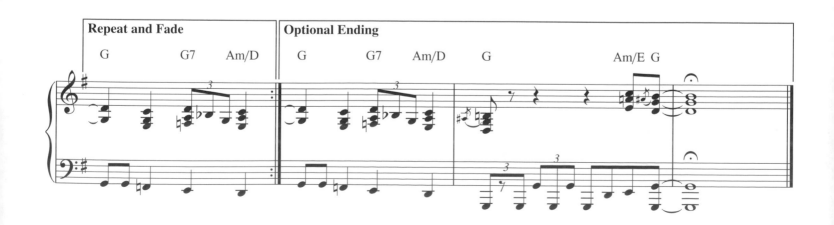

LET IT SNOW! LET IT SNOW! LET IT SNOW!

Words by SAMMY CAHN
Music by JULE STYNE

MERRY CHRISTMAS, DARLING

Words and Music by RICHARD CARPENTER
and FRANK POOLER

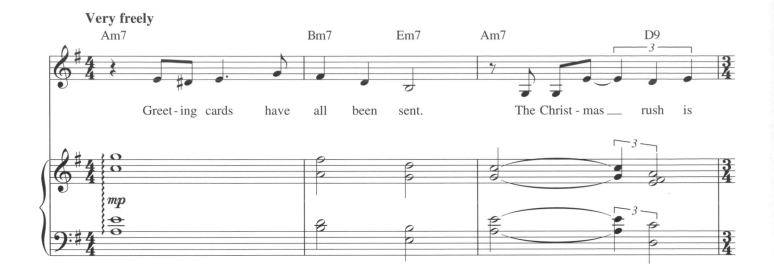

Greet-ing cards have all been sent. The Christ-mas rush is

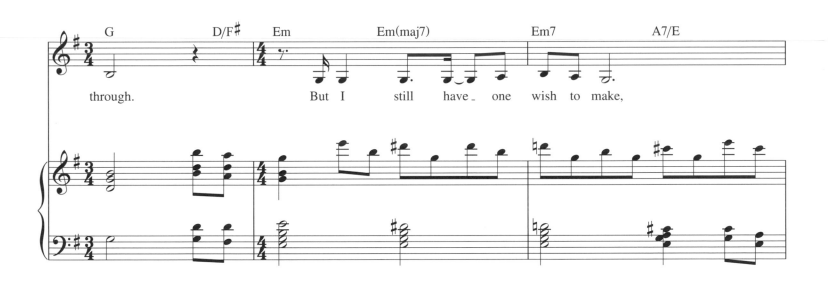

through. But I still have one wish to make, a spe-cial one for you:

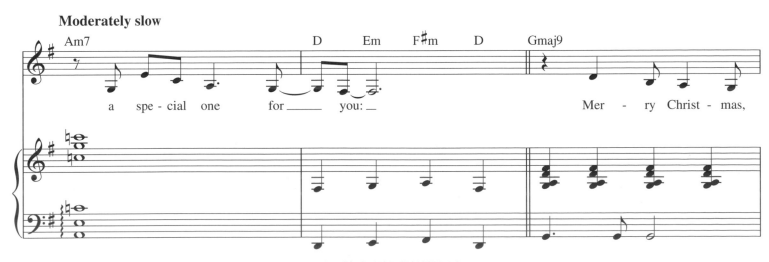

Mer-ry Christ-mas,

THE MOST WONDERFUL TIME OF THE YEAR

Words and Music by EDDIE POLA
and GEORGE WYLE

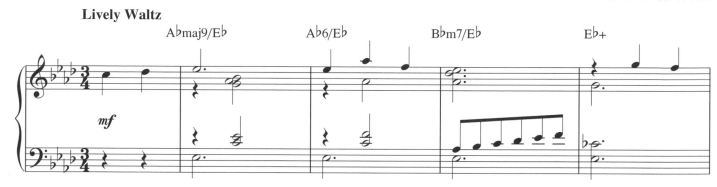

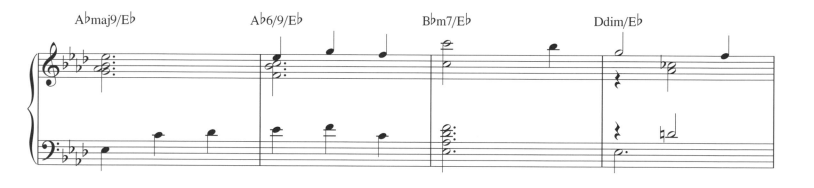

It's the

most won - der - ful time of the

year.

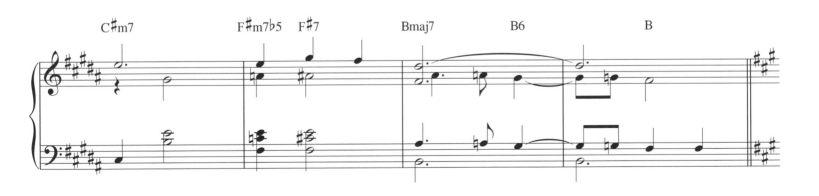

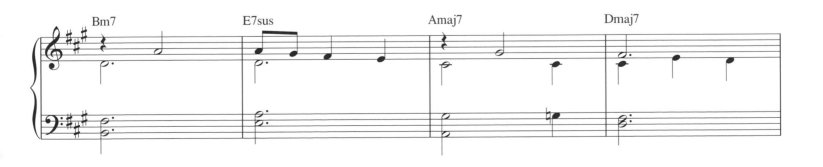

150

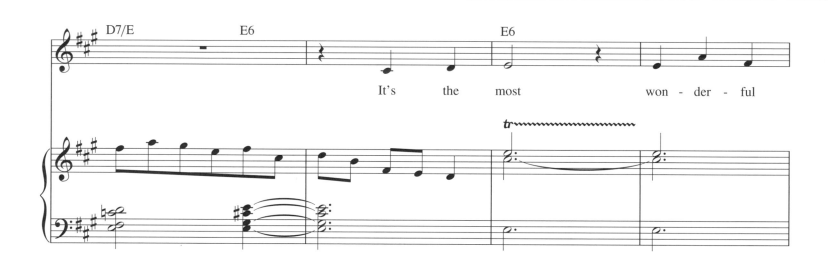

It's   the   most   won - der - ful

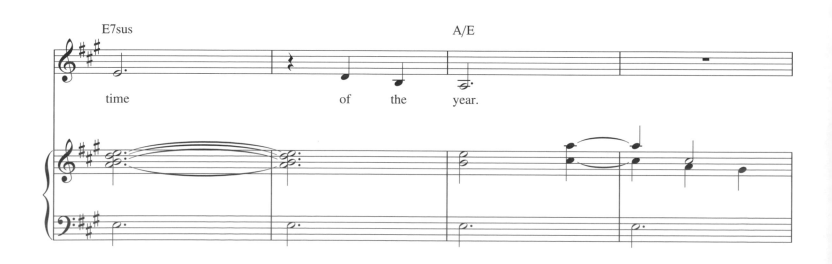

time   of   the   year.

MY FAVORITE THINGS

from THE SOUND OF MUSIC

Lyrics by OSCAR HAMMERSTEIN II
Music by RICHARD RODGERS

Moderate Waltz

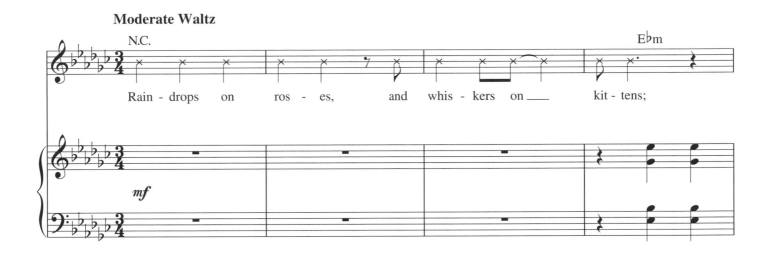

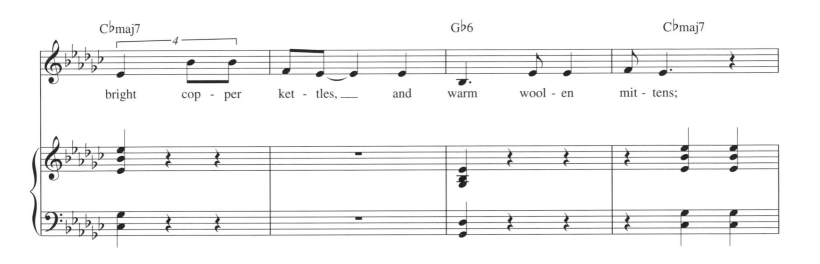

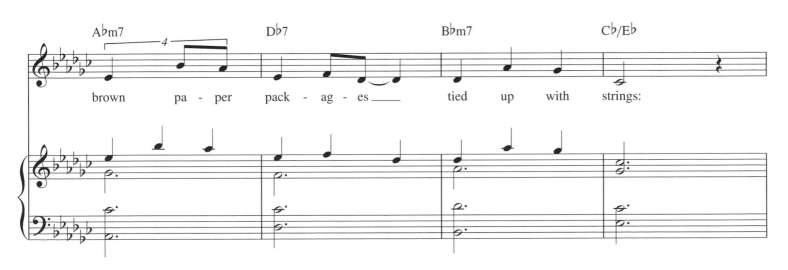

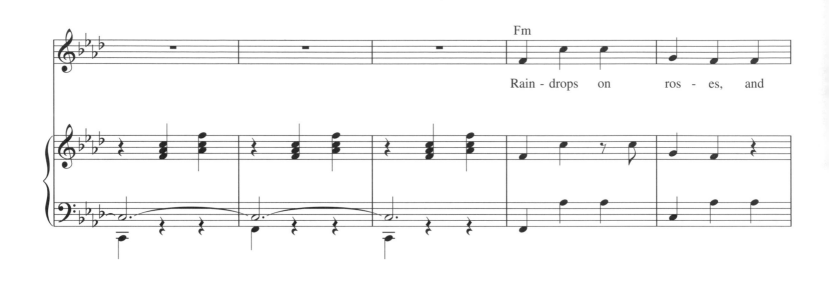

Rain - drops on ros - es, and

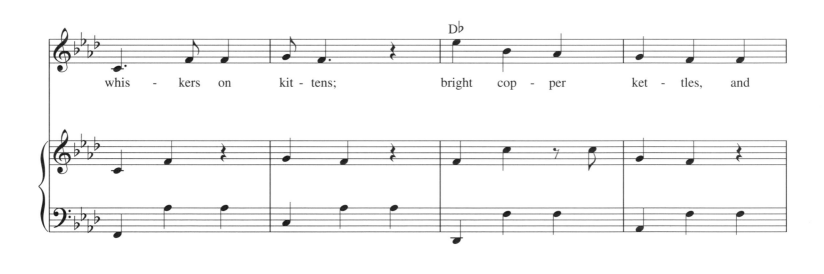

whis - kers on kit - tens; bright cop - per ket - tles, and

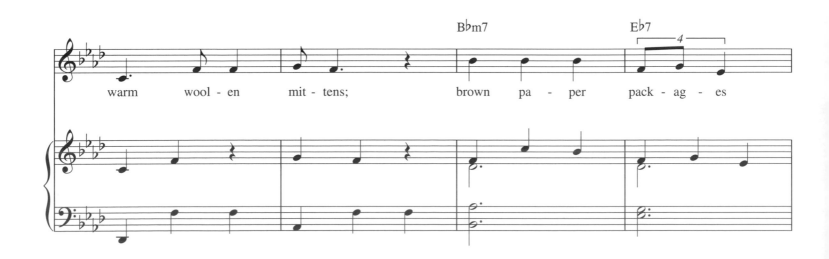

warm wool - en mit - tens; brown pa - per pack - ag - es

ROCKIN' AROUND THE CHRISTMAS TREE

Music and Lyrics by
JOHNNY MARKS

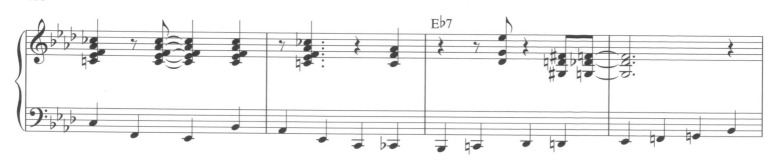

mer - ri - ly in the new old fash - ioned _ way.

RUDOLPH THE RED-NOSED REINDEER

Music and Lyrics by
JOHNNY MARKS

Rubato

SANTA BABY

By JOAN JAVITS,
PHIL SPRINGER and TONY SPRINGER

San - ta, ba - by, just ___
San - ta, ba - by, a

___ slip a sa - ble un - der the ___ tree ___ for ___ me. ___
'fif - ty - four con - ver - ti - ble ___ too— ___ light ___ blue. ___

Been an aw - ful good girl, ___
I'll wait up for you, dear, ___
San - ta, ba - by, so

SANTA CLAUS IS COMIN' TO TOWN

Words by HAVEN GILLESPIE
Music BY J. FRED COOTS

Well, I just got back from a love-ly trip a-long the milk-y way. ___ I

bet-ter watch out, you bet-ter not cry, you bet-ter not pout. I'm a

tell - ing you why: San - ta Claus is com - ing to town.

190

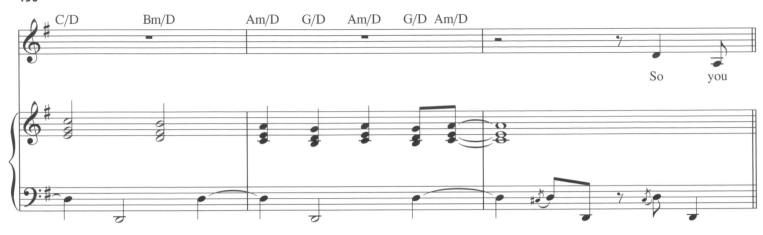

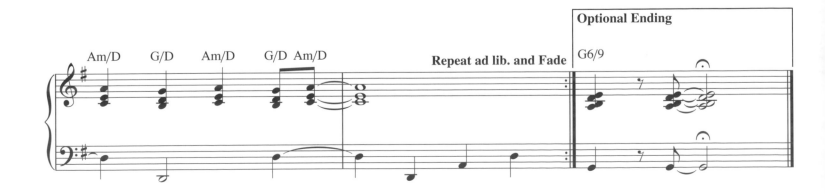

SILVER BELLS
from the Paramount Picture THE LEMON DROP KID

Words and Music by JAY LIVINGSTON
and RAY EVANS

Ring - a - ling, _____ hear them _ ring. _____

Soon it will be Christ - mas day. _____

Steel guitar solo ad lib.

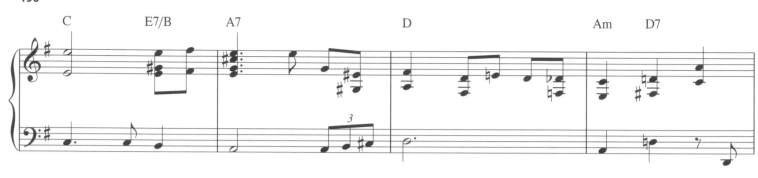

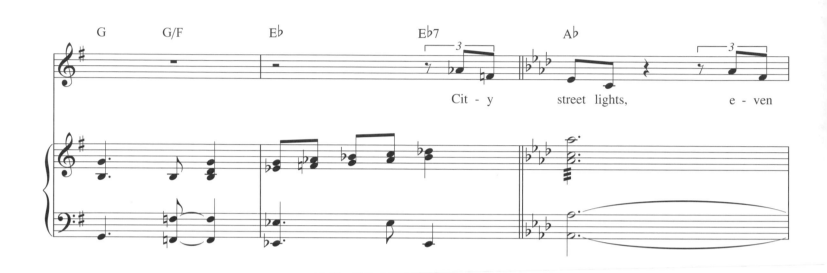

City street lights, e-ven

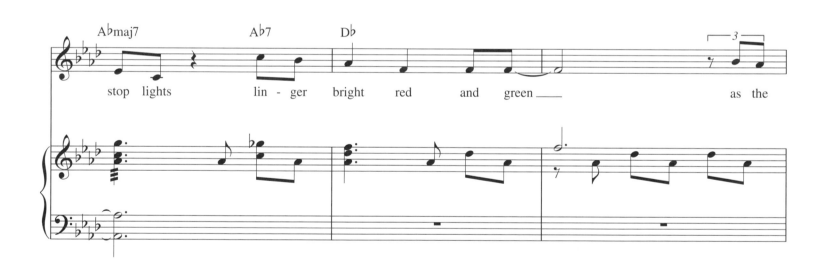

stop lights lin - ger bright red and green _____ as the

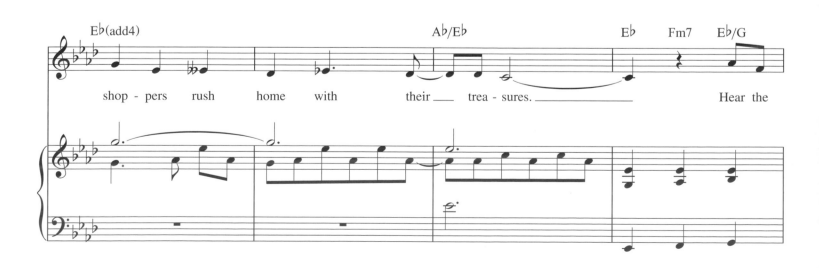

shop - pers rush home with their _____ trea - sures. _____ Hear the

THERE IS NO CHRISTMAS LIKE A HOME CHRISTMAS

Lyrics by CARL SIGMAN
Music by MICKEY ADDY

WHITE CHRISTMAS

from the Motion Picture Irving Berlin's HOLIDAY INN

Words and Music by
IRVING BERLIN

204

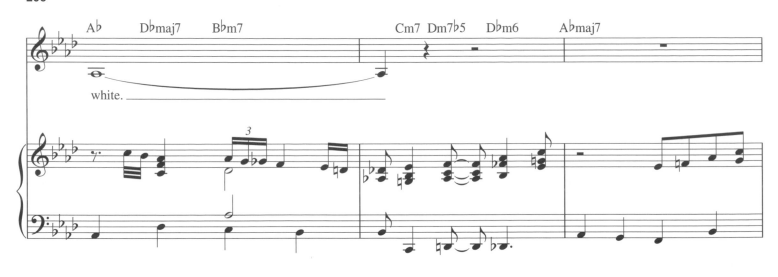

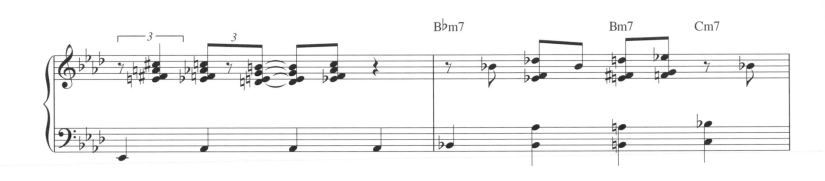

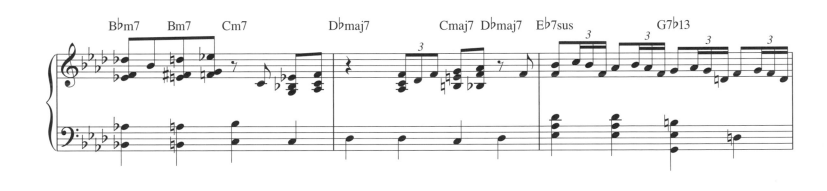

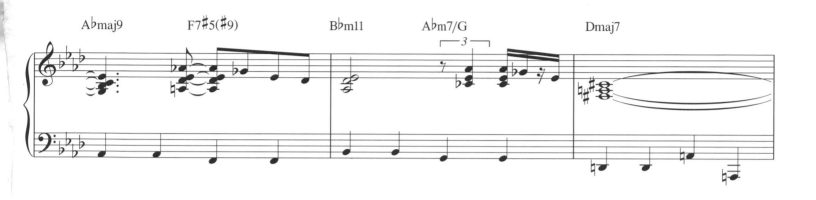

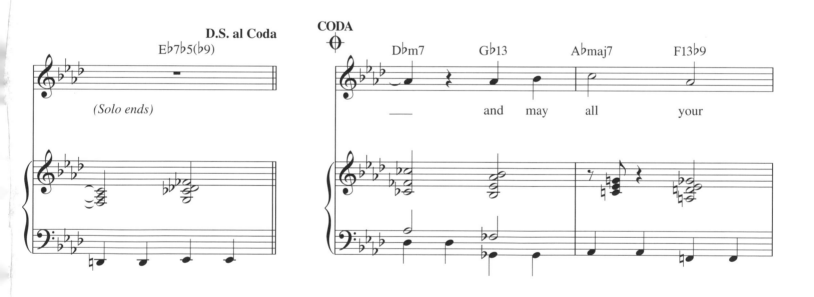

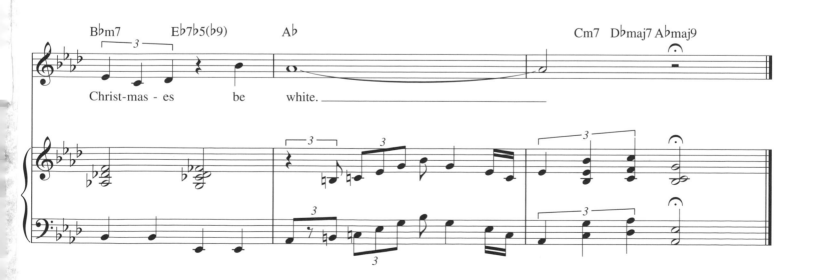

ORIGINAL KEYS FOR SINGERS

ACROSS THE UNIVERSE

Because • Blackbird • Hey Jude • Let It Be • Revolution •
Something • and more.
00307010 Vocal Transcriptions with Piano $19.95

LOUIS ARMSTRONG

Dream a Little Dream of Me • Hello, Dolly! • Mack the Knife
• Makin' Whoopee! • Mame • St. Louis Blues • What a
Wonderful World • Zip-A-Dee-Doo-Dah • and more.
00307029 Vocal Transcriptions with Piano $19.99

MARIAH CAREY

Always Be My Baby • Dreamlover • Emotions •
Heartbreaker • Hero • I Don't Wanna Cry • Love Takes
Time • Loverboy • One Sweet Day • Vision of Love • We
Belong Together • and more.
00306835 Vocal Transcriptions with Piano $19.95

PATSY CLINE

Always • Blue Moon of Kentucky • Crazy • Faded Love
• I Fall to Pieces • Just a Closer Walk with Thee • Sweet
Dreams • more. Also includes a biography.
00740072 Vocal Transcriptions with Piano $15.99

ELLA FITZGERALD

A-tisket, A-tasket • But Not for Me • Easy to Love •
Embraceable You • The Lady Is a Tramp • Misty • Oh,
Lady Be Good! • Satin Doll • Stompin' at the Savoy •
Take the "A" Train • and more. Includes a biography and
discography.
00740252 Vocal Transcriptions with Piano $16.95

JOSH GROBAN

Alejate • Awake • Believe • February Song • In Her Eyes •
Now or Never • O Holy Night • Per Te • The Prayer • To
Where You Are • Un Amore Per Sempre • Un Dia Llegara •
You Are Loved (Don't Give Up) • You Raise Me Up • You're
Still You • and more.
00306969 Vocal Transcriptions with Piano $19.99

GREAT FEMALE SINGERS

Cry Me a River (Ella Fitzgerald) • Crazy (Patsy Cline) •
Fever (Peggy Lee) • How Deep Is the Ocean (How High Is
the Sky) (Billie Holiday) • Little Girl Blue (Nina Simone) •
Tenderly (Rosemary Clooney) • and more.
00307132 Vocal Transcriptions with Piano $19.99

www.halleonard.com

Prices, contents, and availability subject to change without notice.

GREAT MALE SINGERS

Can't Help Falling in Love (Elvis Presley) • Georgia on My
Mind (Ray Charles) • I've Got the World on a String (Frank
Sinatra) • Mona Lisa (Nat King Cole) • Ol' Man River (Paul
Robeson) • What a Wonderful World (Louis Armstrong)
• and more.
00307133 Vocal Transcriptions with Piano $19.99

BILLIE HOLIDAY

Transcribed from Historic Recordings

Billie's Blues (I Love My Man) • Body and Soul • Crazy He
Calls Me • Easy Living • A Fine Romance • God Bless' the
Child • Lover, Come Back to Me • Miss Brown to You •
Strange Fruit • The Very Thought of You • and more.
00740140 Vocal Transcriptions with Piano $16.95

NANCY LAMOTT

Autumn Leaves • Downtown • I Have Dreamed • It Might
as Well Be Spring • Moon River • Skylark • That Old Black
Magic • and more.
00306995 Vocal Transcriptions with Piano $19.99

LEONA LEWIS – SPIRIT

Better in Time • Bleeding Love • The First Time Ever I Saw
Your Face • Here I Am • Homeless • I Will Be • I'm You •
Whatever It Takes • Yesterday • and more.
00307007 Vocal Transcriptions with Piano $17.95

THE BETTE MIDLER SONGBOOK

Boogie Woogie Bugle Boy • Friends • From a Distance
• The Glory of Love • The Rose • Some People's Lives •
Stay with Me • Stuff like That There • Ukulele Lady • The
Wind Beneath My Wings • and more, plus a fantastic bio
and photos.
00307067 Vocal Transcriptions with Piano $19.99

THE BEST OF LIZA MINNELLI

And All That Jazz • Cabaret • Losing My Mind • Maybe This
Time • Me and My Baby • Theme from "New York, New
York" • Ring Them Bells • Sara Lee • Say Liza (Liza with
a Z) • Shine It On • Sing Happy • The Singer • Taking a
Chance on Love.
00306928 Vocal Transcriptions with Piano $19.99

FRANK SINATRA – MORE OF HIS BEST

Almost like Being in Love • Cheek to Cheek • The Days of
Wine and Roses • Fly Me to the Moon • I Could Write a Book
• In the Wee Small Hours of the Morning • It Might as Well
Be Spring • Luck Be a Lady • Old Devil Moon • Somebody
Loves Me • When the World Was Young • and more.
00307081 Vocal Transcriptions with Piano $19.99

THE VERY BEST OF FRANK SINATRA

Come Fly with Me • I've Got You Under My Skin • It Was a
Very Good Year • My Way • Night and Day • Summer Wind
• The Way You Look Tonight • You Make Me Feel So Young
• and more. Includes biography.
00306753 Vocal Transcriptions with Piano $19.95

STEVE TYRELL – BACK TO BACHARACH

Alfie • Always Something There to Remind Me • Close to
You • I Say a Little Prayer • The Look of Love • Raindrops
Keep Fallin' on My Head • This Guy's in Love with You •
Walk on By • and more.
00307024 Vocal Transcriptions with Piano $16.99

THE BEST OF STEVE TYRELL

Ain't Misbehavin' • Fly Me to the Moon (In Other Words) •
Give Me the Simple Life • I Concentrate on You • I've Got
a Crush on You • In the Wee Small Hours of the Morning •
Isn't It Romantic? • A Kiss to Build a Dream On • Stardust
• The Way You Look Tonight • What a Little Moonlight Can
Do • You'd Be So Nice to Come Home To • and more.
00307027 Vocal Transcriptions with Piano $16.99

SARAH VAUGHAN

Black Coffee • If You Could See Me Now • It Might as
Well Be Spring • My Funny Valentine • The Nearness of
You • A Night in Tunisia • Perdido • September Song •
Tenderly • and more.
00306558 Vocal Transcriptions with Piano $17.95

ANDY WILLIAMS – CHRISTMAS COLLECTION

Blue Christmas • The Christmas Song (Chestnuts Roasting
on an Open Fire) • Do You Hear What I Hear • Happy
Holiday • Kay Thompson's Jingle Bells • The Little
Drummer Boy • The Most Wonderful Time of the Year • O
Holy Night • Sleigh Ride • What Are You Doing New Year's
Eve? • and more. Includes a great bio!
00307158 Vocal Transcriptions with Piano $17.99

ANDY WILLIAMS

Can't Get Used to Losing You • The Days of Wine and Roses •
The Hawaiian Wedding Song (Ke Kali Nei Au) • The Impossible
Dream • Moon River • More • The Most Wonderful Time of
the Year • Red Roses for a Blue Lady • Speak Softly, Love • A
Time for Us • Where Do I Begin • and more.
00307160 Vocal Transcriptions with Piano $17.99